MARRIAGETODAY™
P.O. Box 59888
Dallas, TX 75229

800-380-6330
www.marriagetoday.com

Typeset in Brix Slab and Futura Std
Design, illustrations, and photography by This Paper Ship
www.thispapership.com

ISBN: 978-0-578-09382-6

Second Printing
Printed in the United States of America by Carter Printing & Graphics, Inc., Knightdale, NC

10 9 8 7 6 5 4 3 2

What are the ingredients of a healthy marriage? Ask a dozen married couples and you're likely to get a dozen different answers. Love and respect. Mutual attraction. Shared interests. Good conversation. Passion and romance. Unconditional love. All of these are legitimate responses. Each of these creates satisfaction and well-being in a relationship—and that sense of delight in one's spouse is essential to a good marriage.

So why don't more couples delight in each other? Why aren't more marriages happier? What happened to the joy that filled the space between you during your courtship, wedding ceremony, and honeymoon?

Our focus at MarriageToday is helping couples succeed in marriage. We see far too many relationships crumble due to nothing more than simple distraction. It's so easy to have our attention pulled away from each other and toward other (good) things, like work or kids. How do you restore the romance? How do you rejuvenate the joy?

There's no easy fix, but we've seen many marriages revitalized when husbands and wives recommit themselves to the little things that make a relationship sing—thoughtfulness, acts of kindness, genuine affection, honest sharing, and regular dates or opportunities to get away together.

Re-introduce the little things to your relationship and the bigger issues begin to fall in line.

This little book is full of little things—romance tips, date night ideas, actions to take and decisions to make—designed to re-infuse your marriage with joy.

In his nineteenth-century poem, "Ode on a Grecian Urn," the poet John Keats composed a line that fills us with joy every time we think of it: "More happy love! / more happy, happy love!" Whether you read a chapter a day, a chapter a week, or the whole thing in one delightful sitting, we hope the tips and suggestions in this book lead to an overflow of happy, happy love between you and your spouse.

When I was a child, my parents' marriage almost ended in divorce. That's not an exaggeration. Things were desperate, and they barely escaped becoming another statistic. They had to rebuild their relationship from the ground up, but eventually found reconciliation. Today, after over 40 years together, Jimmy and Karen Evans are still enjoying a fruitful, healthy marriage. If their marriage could be saved, they reasoned, anyone's could—and that's why they dedicated themselves to helping other couples learn and apply the principles that saved their own marriage.

Jimmy and Karen founded MarriageToday in 1994, believing troubled marriages could get better, and good marriages could become great. Since then, using books, seminars, and a national television program (*MarriageToday with Jimmy & Karen*), they've coached thousands of couples toward restoring marriages and building healthy homes.

I've seen it in their lives and I've seen it in my own marriage: Great marriages don't happen by chance. They require nurture and training. They require the intentional actions of romance, scheduled date nights, and other relationship-building endeavors like those mentioned in this book. It takes effort. That's why we're committed to giving husbands and wives the tools they need to build a strong marriage. We hope this fun little book has helped do just that.

May your marriage be filled with "happy, happy love."

Brenton L. Evans

Brenton Evans
President, MarriageToday

Brenton and Stephanie Evans

GET ROMANTIC

Find something your husband or wife has used to oblivion and secretly replace it with a shiny new one. How long until he or she finds out? (Drop little hints if necessary, or drop a gigantic hint by garnishing it with a big red bow.)

LOVE LESSON

Even when you disagree, do it calmly. Be respectful and keep your voice level. Nagging, yelling, or whining do more harm than good.

DATE NIGHT

Plan ahead. Purchase several restaurant gift cards for places you love. Head out. After you've traveled a block or two—without looking—choose one of the gift cards. Then enjoy your meal at a surprise location.

Romance

is a self-initiated pursuit. It means doing something

special *for your* spouse

without any begging or coaxing.

— Jimmy Evans

GET ROMANTIC

Make a list of the five things you like most about your spouse. Share them with him/her via one sticky-note each day this week. Bonus points if you hide the notes somewhere new every time. (Ideas: attach a note to her steering wheel, stick one inside one of his shoes, secure one beneath her coffee mug.)

LOVE LESSON

How many times a day do you hug your spouse? How often do you kiss or say "I love you"? Keep count for a day, then improve on that number the day after... and the day after that.

DEEPER

Think about your relationship 20 years from now. What do you hope your marriage looks like? How will it have deepened? What do you think will have changed? Discuss with each other.

Go to the library. Find an old cookbook. Browse through it together, pick out an interesting dish, then copy the recipe and ingredients. Go shop for those ingredients. Head home and cook it up. Dine with the fancy dishes and candlelight.

MRS BEETON COOKER

...oking

...MBE

...RAHMBOMBE

...ream into three portions,
...neal or raspberry jelly,
...e, adding marachino,
...cherry liqueur and mix

...gelatine and add a third
...ns.

...into a tall glass mould.
...hen the raspberry and
... in a refrigerator until
...h whipped cream and

...G WITH APPLES
...UF

...ten egg whites
... sugar
...of half a lemon
...ta flavouring

...rind to the boil, then
...minutes. Draw to the
...h and a lid, and leave
...he milk. Remove the

...ter together, add the

Desserts

Peel, slice and parboil the apples. Arrange ...
apples and rice in alternate layers in a greased casserole, ...
spread with the creamed egg and butter, and bake in a
moderate oven for half an hour.

BAKED APPLE PUDDING
APFELAUFLAUF

2 lb. cooking apples
4 oz. sugar
4 oz. flour
2 eggs

grated rind of one lemon
3 oz. blanched and chopped
    almonds

Peel and slice the apples and arrange in the bottom of
greased casserole. Sprinkle with sugar and almonds.
Mix the eggs and the flour to a batter, and pour over
the apples. Add the lemon juice and bake in a moderate
oven until the apples are tender and the batter has set
and browned.

COTTAGE CHEESE
AND STRAWBERRIES
QUARK MIT ERDBEEREN

½ lb. cottage cheese
½ lb. strawberries or raspberries
1 cup whipped cream

grated rind of half a lemon
2 oz. sugar
1 teaspoon rum

Rub the cheese through a sieve and mix with the cream.
Add the lemon rind, rum and sugar. Arrange in a pile,
pyramid shaped, and surround with strawberries. Serve
with thin wafer biscuits.

GET ROMANTIC

Most women love roses. Guys don't mind them either. But let's be honest: they're a bit of a romantic cliché. Avoid the formulaic romance and bring home a single flower that's not a rose. (For a list of alternatives to the red rose, check out page 46.)

LOVE LESSON

Sometimes it's easier to withdraw during a conflict—or to make accusations—but the best approach is almost always to say "I'm sorry." The strongest marriages are the ones in which both spouses race to be the first to apologize.

3

DATE NIGHT

Can't afford a weekend away? Send the kids to a sitter's or their grandparents' for the night. Move your mattress into a different room of your home. See what happens.

Date nights are wonderful, but don't forget to find unstructured time to hang out with your spouse. Relax together. Laugh and have fun. Be spontaneous. Find new and creative ways to enjoy each other's company.

Relax

GET ROMANTIC

Set a daily reminder on your phone or calendar to either call or text your spouse, just to connect during the day. No need for anything fancy. If you're texting, just tap out a quick "Thinking of you" or "I love you." (Hint: Check your spelling, because "I liver you" will only cause confusion and embarrassment.)

LOVE LESSON

Every time you get annoyed with your spouse's bad habits, first take a moment to examine your own flaws and address them. Think of it as precautionary marital maintenance.

4

DEEPER

Every married person should be familiar enough with their spouse's favorite hobby to ask meaningful questions about it. How much do you know about her Pilates classes? How much do you know about his NASCAR obsession? Get educated! Your husband or wife will love you for it.

Visit your local indoor or outdoor miniature golf complex. Play a round, keep score, and make it interesting with a marital wager. For instance, the loser of the round must give a massage to the winner. Or the winner of each hole gets a kiss from the loser (everyone wins!). Keep it competitive!

Winner gets a kiss!

GET ROMANTIC

Flowers? Cards? Chocolates? You can do that for anyone. Do something for your spouse that you wouldn't do for anyone else.

LOVE LESSON

One key to a happy marriage: take care of yourself. Good habits like exercise and healthy eating result in more energy, lower stress, and a better attitude. A healthier spouse means a healthier marriage.

5

DATE NIGHT

Find a local ice cream store within walking distance. Walk there. Buy ice cream cones (bowls not allowed).* Walk back. Eat cones. Hold hands.

* Yes, we realize the advocacy of ice cream might contradict the "healthy living" advice also on this page. But you're allowed to splurge every once in awhile—especially in the name of love.

How to appreciate your spouse,
in three words:
spontaneous shoulder rubs.

shoulder rubs

Some of our favorite date night ideas only work certain times of the year.

Independence Day:

✳ You might not be able to get away from other people, but don't pass up the chance to snuggle in the dark while you watch fireworks.

Halloween:

✳ Is there a cornfield maze near you? Make a date of it. Rule: You must kiss each other every time you reach a dead end.

Thanksgiving:

✳ After Thanksgiving dinner, gain some alone time with your spouse and burn a few calories by taking a walk together. A long walk.

Christmas:

✱ After a romantic dinner, head home, turn off the room lights, turn on the Christmas tree lights, and cuddle on the couch in the twinkly dark.

✱ Take your spouse to a Christmas pageant or production at a local church—especially a church you've never attended.

✱ Schedule an afternoon away from work and go Christmas shopping together.

New Year's:

✱ Go to dinner, with one goal: Together, come up with a list of marriage and/or family resolutions for the coming year.

GET ROMANTIC

Over the course of several days, bring home one flower a day and put it in a vase. Choose different colors and types. By the end of the week, your kitchen table will be sporting a progressive, homemade bouquet! Note: This one's not just for the guys. Once you've started the bouquet, alternate days between the two of you. Who can find the most unique or colorful flower?

LOVE LESSON

When you're falling in love, you pay close attention to the other person. You stay in love by maintaining that attention, year-in and year-out, in your marriage.

6

DATE NIGHT

When was the last time you went to an amusement park without your kids? Go for it. Be adventurous. Ride rides. Hold hands while you walk. Feed each other funnel cake. You'll have more fun than you'd think.

Spend a day noting the way you talk to your spouse—especially your tone of voice. Ask your spouse about it. Do you ever come across as demanding? Whiny? Insensitive? If so, fix it! Pleasant words are like honey (Prov. 16:24). Speak sweetly to each other.

Pleasant words are like HONEY.

Proverbs 16:24

GET ROMANTIC

Start a tradition and stick to it: A whisper every time you leave each other's company. A kiss every night. A hand on the knee when you pray together. A lunch date every week. An overnight trip each month.

LOVE LESSON

At the end of the day, always ask "How was your day?" whether you think you know the answer or not. Part of it is courtesy. Part of it is communication. Make it a habit.

7

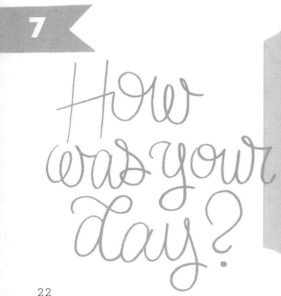

DEEPER

The things you think are romantic don't necessarily have the same impact on your spouse. Look through his or her eyes first.

If it's not romantic to your husband or wife, it's not romantic. Period.

Go to your favorite restaurant but follow this rule: each of you has to order something you've never tried before. Embrace the adventure!

GET ROMANTIC

Think of something you like about your spouse. Write it on a sticky note. Tonight, put it where he or she will find it in the morning.

LOVE LESSON

It's healthy to be honest about what bothers you, but don't forget to also communicate the positive stuff. When you're grateful, say it. Even more importantly, show it.

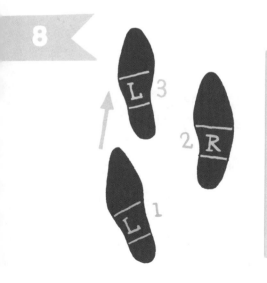

8

DATE NIGHT

Take a dance class together at the local community center or junior college. Swing, ballroom, tango: it's a built-in date night once a week.

When

romance

is alive and well
in a marriage, the door of

TEMPTATION

gets

slammed shut.

—Jimmy Evans

GET ROMANTIC

Practical gifts: A bad choice for Valentine's Day, but outstanding when it comes to romantic surprises. Is there something your husband or wife really needs? Bring one home today.

LOVE LESSON

In his play, *Two Gentlemen of Verona,* one of Shakespeare's characters says: "They do not love who do not show their love." Love is best expressed through actions. Forsooth: How have you showed love to your spouse today?

They do not LOVE who do not SHOW their love

DEEPER

The most romantic gestures are the ones that show your spouse you've been paying attention—and you know them well. Are you a good observer of your spouse?

DATE NIGHT

Try something new! Attend a sporting event you've never seen live. Tennis match? Golf tournament? Tractor pull?

GET ROMANTIC

Gentlemen: You know your wife's favorite fragrance, right? (Please say yes.) Surprise her with something in that aromatic family, like soap, lotion, or candles.

Wives: He might not be interested in a frou-frou lotion, but he'd love a gift card to his favorite store. Surprise him with one hidden in his car, briefcase, or wallet. Attach a note that says "I love you."

LOVE LESSON

Here's an important phrase to repeat, memorize, and bring to mind on a regular basis, appropriate for both husbands and wives: *I am not always right.*

10

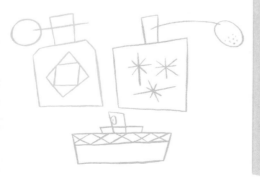

DEEPER

The more familiar we get with someone, the more our manners degrade. Are you as polite to your spouse now as when you were dating? Are you doing the things you used to do to make yourself attractive? Are you still working overtime to impress your husband or wife?

DATE NIGHT

Dress down, gear up, and go camping at the local state park (or set up your tent in the backyard). Observe the night sky. Toast marshmallows over a fire, a candle, or a grill. Zip together your sleeping bags and snuggle.

GET ROMANTIC

What's her favorite coffee or tea? What's his favorite snack or dessert? Pick it up on a random day and surprise your spouse at work or home.

LOVE LESSON

The best marriages are the ones in which both husband and wife act as if their spouse is far better than they deserved.

11

DATE NIGHT

Schedule a pedicure together. Yes, including the husband. Odds are he needs one... and he'll enjoy it more than he thinks.

2
BE
romantic

Want more romance in your marriage? Then be romantic. It starts with you.

GET ROMANTIC

You've heard of "drinking games," right? That's when fans of popular TV shows watch while on the lookout for certain catchphrases or regularly repeated actions. When a character says or does something within the rules of the game, the participants take a drink. We're no fans of binge drinking, but what if you transformed it into a kissing game? Find an online list of drinking game rules for your favorite show—there are plenty—but kiss your spouse instead of taking a drink. Who says watching TV has to be an isolating experience?

LOVE LESSON

Above all, be kind and considerate to your spouse. Thoughtfulness goes a long way.

12

DATE NIGHT

Have a non-procrastination night. Order pizza. Then, together, do the things around the house you've been putting off. Stop between chores for a long hug, a slow dance, or a make-out session.

Always take the time to praise your spouse when he or she puts effort into something, regardless of the situation.

the quotable marriage

"I want to be with my best friend, and my best friend's my wife. Who could ask for anything more?"

—John Lennon

"Let the wife make the husband glad to come home, and let him make her sorry to see him leave."

—Martin Luther

"To get the full value of joy you must have someone to divide it with."

—Mark Twain

"By all means marry. If you get a good wife you will become happy, and if you get a bad one you will become a philosopher."

—Socrates

"What a happy and holy fashion it is that those who love one another should rest on the same pillow."
  —Nathaniel Hawthorne

"The heart of marriage is memories."
  —Bill Cosby

"Marriage is the hardest thing you will ever do. The secret is removing divorce as an option. Anybody who gives themselves that option will get a divorce."
  —Will Smith

"My wife tells me that if I ever decide to leave, she is coming with me."
  —Jon Bon Jovi

"The first bond of society is marriage."
  —Cicero

The heart of a marriage is memories. —Bill Cosby

GET ROMANTIC

Search online for "glow-in-the-dark adhesive stars" or ask for them at your local toy store. Buy a set. Secretly spell out "I Love You" on the ceiling above your bed. Surprise!

LOVE LESSON

Do you make eye contact with him or her during conversations? Not doing so makes you seem distracted or, worse, a little devious. Take notice of your own habits, and adjust them if necessary.

13

DATE NIGHT

Make plans with another couple (preferably one you know well). This week, they prepare and serve you a romantic meal at their place. Next week, you and your spouse return the favor.

When you initiate romance in your marriage relationship, you communicate to your spouse that he or she is

desirable

to you.

— Jimmy Evans

GET ROMANTIC

When you hug your spouse, which of you is the first to let go? Next time the two of you embrace, try to be the one who hugs longest. Frequent daily hugs have a measurable benefit for women. Researchers have found that it boosts blood levels of the feel-good hormone oxytocin, which can lower blood pressure. (Men don't get the same benefit, but they'll enjoy the hugs all the same.)

LOVE LESSON

Do unto others as you would have them do unto you. Want a back rub? Offer your spouse one.

14

our BUDGET

DEEPER

If you don't have one already, sit down with your spouse and make a budget. Talk it through. Prioritize. Don't be one of those couples who are always fighting about money. (If you need help in this area, Dave Ramsey's *Total Money Makeover* or *Financial Peace Planner* are great places to start. And though we're a teensy bit biased, the audio CD series "You, Me & Money" from MarriageToday is a great resource, too.)

DATE NIGHT

Make it a progressive dinner:
Enjoy appetizers at one restaurant,
the full meal at another, then make
one more stop for dessert or coffee.

GET ROMANTIC

Guys, whenever possible, open the door for your wife. Ladies, whenever possible, find a way to return the favor. He may not allow you to open doors for him—some guys would find that awkward—but look for opportunities to practice a similar kind of "after you" graciousness.

LOVE LESSON

The next time you intend to say something critical to your spouse, just don't. For once, delete it and let the incident pass without comment.

15

DATE NIGHT

Dollar date night: Each of you buys a gift for the other from the local dollar or discount store. Wrap it. Open each other's gifts, then pick up dinner from a fast-food dollar-menu. Find a secluded, romantic place to eat and enjoy all the money you saved.

Share your expectations with your spouse about things like finances, parenting, upcoming plans, household duties, etc. This prevents future arguments and protects you both from disappointment.

GET ROMANTIC

Have you ever given your husband or wife a face massage? Trust us: you'll both enjoy it. Gently massage the cheeks and jaw in an upward direction, toward the forehead. Always massage in the direction of a smile—never into a frown.

LOVE LESSON

Two words that should never be said in a healthy marriage: "Me first." (Unless you're doing something dangerous.)

DEEPER

Sure, you remember your wedding anniversary. But do you remember the anniversary of when you first met? Or when you got engaged? Sit down with your spouse and walk through some of the significant events of your burgeoning relationship. Then remember those dates and celebrate them next year.

Find a movie you both loved when you were teenagers, and watch it again together. Talk about the first time you saw the film. What were the circumstances? Who were you with? What did you think about it back then? How does your "grown-up" opinion of it compare to your teenage perspective?

ZANY 1960's SCREWBALL FLICK

18th-Century English Romance

CHILDHOOD ANIMATED CLASSIC

GRITTY but ENDEARING Western

QUIRKY Romantic COMEDY

Vintage 1980's Favorite

OBSCURE but UNDERRATED 1990's MOVIE

SUPERHERO TRIUMPH

Fantasy with Wizards, Elves, & Dwarves

GET ROMANTIC

Next time you have to travel on business, write your spouse a card or note for every day you'll be gone. Leave the set behind in a conspicuous place, with "To be opened on (date)" clearly labeled on each one.

LOVE LESSON

Husbands: Sometimes cuddling needs to just be cuddling, instead of the first road toward a certain, uh, destination.

Wives: Try not to be too annoyed when your guy seems to view everything as some kind of foreplay. Because to him, everything pretty much is foreplay.

17

DATE NIGHT

DIY Frisbee® Golf. Go to a local park. Identify landmarks (trees, signs, tables) and see who can reach them with the fewest throws of a flying disc. Keep score!

DEEPER

What you are willing to give up for your *spouse* shows how much you think he or she is *worth.*

— Jimmy Evans

Nine alternatives to the traditional red rose

Roses are red... and fairly routine, when it comes to romance. Ditch the formula and bring your spouse one of these:

* **Carnation** (long-lasting and fragrant)
* **Daisy** (these are the "he loves me, he loves me not" flower!)
* **Daffodil** (known for its sweet fragrance)
* **Freesia** (long considered a symbol of trust and faithfulness)
* **Gladiolus** (the name comes from the Latin word for sword. Tell the recipient of these spear-shaped blooms that she has "pierced" your heart, but in a way that doesn't make you seem like some lame pick-up artist.)
* **Lilac** (heart-shaped leaves)
* **Lily** (star-shaped blooms represent beauty and devotion)
* **Sunflower** (symbolizes warmth, happiness, and loyalty)
* **Tulip** (some identify these as the most romantic flowers)

Carnation

Lily

Daisy

Freesia

Tulip

Gladiolus

GET ROMANTIC

Why do married couples always do that quick peck-on-the-cheek thing? Were you satisfied with chaste pecking before you got married? No? Then don't settle for it now! Before you leave the house tomorrow, plant a big one on your spouse. Linger.

LOVE LESSON

Look for opportunities during the day to show gratitude. Whether it's a verbal "thank you" or even a handwritten thank-you note, make sure your spouse knows how appreciated he or she is. Nothing strengthens a relationship like sincere thankfulness.

18

DEEPER

Men: Tell your wife "I love you" out of the blue today. Pick an unexpected time. Then do this every day for the rest of your life.

Women: Say "I'm proud of you" to your husband today. Do it privately. Do it in public. Do it again tomorrow, and the day after that.

Rent a tandem bike at the park or beach. Make sure you alternate who gets the better view. (Is the "better view" from the front or back? That's up to you!) Also: wear helmets. And choose a good steerer.

GET ROMANTIC

Save electricity! After the kids go to bed, light the house with candlelight.

LOVE LESSON

Don't criticize your husband or wife in front of other people — including your children. On the flip side, when was the last time you complimented your spouse in public? Be generous with the praise in front of your kids, in front of your friends, and even among strangers.

19

DATE NIGHT

Barefoot Date Night: Take a picnic meal to a park. Bring a blanket to sit on. Remove your shoes when you arrive. Don't put them back on until you leave.

You may make a lot of

MONEY

but if your job keeps you
from your family,
the things it buys won't solve
your marriage problems.

— Jimmy Evans

GET ROMANTIC

Next time you borrow his or her usual car, take it to the car wash. Vacuum it. Fill the tank. Wipe down the dash. De-clutter. Or just splurge and get the car detailed. Then keep it a secret.

LOVE LESSON

You're a single married unit, but the unit is made of two unique individuals—one of whom you fell in love with. Don't forget to allow each spouse the room to be themselves.

20

DEEPER

Set aside time at the end of every day for the two of you to just talk. When you do, be honest and open. Share information. Talk about your day, your worries, your goals for the future. You'll both come to enjoy it.

When was the last time you had your photo taken together—just the two of you? Hire a local photographer, dress up, and have fun!

GET ROMANTIC

Spend time this week thinking about the things in life that make your spouse smile. Then spend the next week bringing those things into his or her life.

LOVE LESSON

Do you find yourself constantly dwelling on your spouse's failures? The next time you're tempted to complain or criticize, stop to make a list of his or her best qualities. Bring those up instead.

21

DATE NIGHT

Stay at home and play the classic "Board Games + Back Rub." What, you haven't heard of it? Pick out one of your favorite two-person games, like Battleship, Connect Four or chess. Play each other. Whoever wins the most games gets a massage from the loser.

Or for another type of friendly wager, try a combination bowling and movie night. Whoever has the highest bowling score gets to pick the movie.

Here's a paradox worth remembering: as a couple your most romantic moments will often occur when you're not trying to be romantic.

3 words to re-energize your marriage.

Add some zest to your relationship with any of these three-word suggestions:

* Backyard candlelit dinner
* Impromptu foot rub
* Fancy night out
* Compliment each other
* Inside floor picnic
* Public affection display
* Long slow dance
* Improve your appearance
* Mail handwritten notes
* Pamper your spouse
* Surprise weekend away

Fun facts about kissing

Bet you didn't know that...

* The science of kissing is known as *philematology*.
* No, really, there is actually such a thing as "the science of kissing."
* There are one hundred times more nerve endings in your lips than in your fingertips.
* Two out of every three couples tilt their heads to the right for a passionate kiss (but it has nothing to do with being right-handed).
* Frequent kissing has been shown to improve circulation, relieve headaches, and help prevent tooth decay.
* Kissing activates nearly three dozen facial muscles.
* Studies have shown that people remember more details from a first kiss than a first sexual experience.
* Two-thirds of people always keep their eyes closed while kissing. This might be related to the fact that a passionate kiss can actually make your pupils dilate.
* In our brains, kissing releases dopamine, a "reward" neurotransmitter. Addictive drugs like cocaine and nicotine also stimulate the release of dopamine.
* A one-minute kiss can burn up to 26 calories.

GET ROMANTIC

Get a dry erase marker—preferably a red one—and regularly leave notes for your spouse on the bathroom mirror. Suggestions:

- I love you
- You look beautiful
- Have a great day!
- Thinking about you today...
- Hey—put some clothes on!

LOVE LESSON

Stop trying to change your husband or wife. That's not your job. Instead, figure out what you need to change about yourself... and do it.

22

DEEPER

Love is a feeling. Romance is the action taken as a result of that feeling. What have you done today to show your spouse that you love him or her?

Rent a canoe or paddleboat at a nearby lake. Nothing beats the silence and isolation of being out on the water together.

GET ROMANTIC

Next time it rains, grab an umbrella and go for a walk together. Extra points for stomping in puddles, or straight-up making out in the rain like that scene from *The Notebook*.

LOVE LESSON

Don't be afraid of time spent alone or apart from your spouse. Healthy couples allow each other to pursue hobbies and interests, and (of course) absence makes the heart grow fonder. Just don't go crazy with the "me time." Good marriages result from couples who enjoy each other's company and do stuff together. Doesn't matter what you're doing. Doesn't matter if you have kids or not. It just matters that you're together.

23

DATE NIGHT

Visit a bookstore or the public library, and each of you pick out a book for the other. Discuss why you made that choice. Use it as a conversation starter about your favorite books, authors, topics, and other reading preferences.

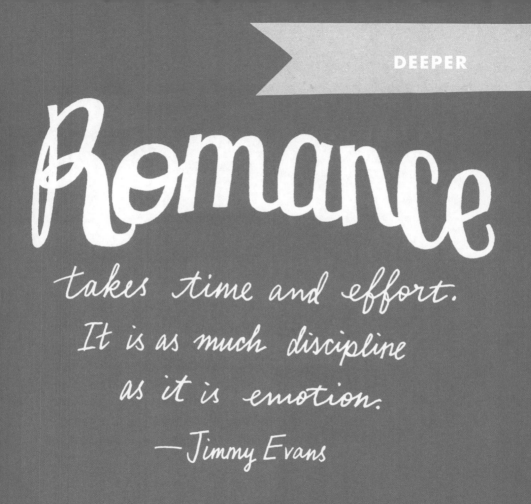

DEEPER

Romance

takes time and effort.
It is as much discipline
as it is emotion.

— Jimmy Evans

GET ROMANTIC

Pick out a book you'll both enjoy and spend every night for the next couple of weeks reading aloud to each other. (Or, if you pick this book, every night for the next few days. And make sure you show each other the pictures!)

LOVE LESSON

Never threaten divorce, whether you mean it or not. Never. Don't even use the word, even if your goal is just to get your spouse's attention. There are much better ways to get his or her attention. For example: nudity.

24

DATE NIGHT

When was the last time you watched the day end together? Make dinner plans with the intent on finishing up by sunset. Park somewhere with an unobstructed view. Enjoy the show. One rule: No kissing until the sun has totally disappeared. At that point, have at it!

Romance

isn't something we do for ourselves

it's something we do for our

spouses.

— Jimmy Evans

GET ROMANTIC

Get a blanket, put the kids to bed, and snuggle on the porch. You are required to kiss if you see a shooting star. You are required to kiss if you see a satellite. In fact, you are required to kiss anytime you find yourself snuggling under a blanket with your spouse, regardless of where you are.

LOVE LESSON

* Four words never to say to your spouse: "I told you so."
* Seven words never to say to your spouse: "Yes, that does make you look fat."

25

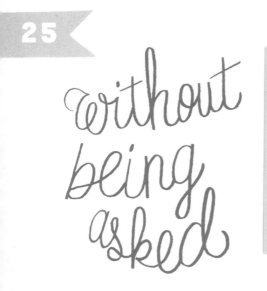

DEEPER

Romance is nothing more than meeting your spouse's unspoken needs or desires. It's doing the stuff you know they'll love—but without being asked.

DATE NIGHT

Find a restaurant within walking distance from your home. Combine a long walk with a romantic meal.

GET ROMANTIC

Do you have a dimmer switch on your bedroom lighting? If not, you should install one. As soon as possible. Seriously. Why are you still reading this?

LOVE LESSON

Do you smile at your spouse? Next time he or she comes home, smile and say "hi." Smile big. Smile with your whole face, including your eyes. Does it feel weird? Then do it every day until it feels normal.

26

DATE NIGHT

Shoulders. Back. Feet. Scalp. Write these on slips of paper, then draw from a hat. Each of you alternate 15-min. massages. Mutual massages aren't a traditional "date," but you'll both love it.

What is one thing you could change, personally, that would improve your marriage?

What keeps you from making that change?

change

Let's be honest: men need help when it comes to romance. Maybe it's because men are less adept with emotions. Maybe it's because guys are more focused on problem-solving. Whatever the reason, the romantic instinct is less developed in the male gender. Regardless, that's no excuse! Here are some tips just for you:

✽ If you haven't done so in awhile, tell your wife she looks beautiful.

✽ But don't just compliment her appearance. Compliment her mind, character, parenting, commitment, etc.

✽ You know that chore she's been asking you to do which you haven't done yet? Do it this weekend.

* While she's bathing, toss her bath towel in the dryer to warm it up. Nothing says "I love you" like a preheated towel. (But make sure you time it right. Nothing says, "my husband is in serious trouble" like a missing towel when she steps out of the shower.)

* Do you still hold the door for her? Pull out her chair at restaurants? Put the toilet seat down? If not...then what's wrong with you? Get to it!

* Sure it feels awkward, but she really does like it when you offer your arm as you're walking together.

* If your wife handles the cooking in your family, she'll be thrilled the next time you tell her not to worry about dinner. Even if it means you're just picking something up on the way home.

* Yes, she wants flowers. She loves it when you bring them to her. But she wants flowers with meaning. Flowers that show you're thinking about her. Grocery-store flowers as an afterthought? A rose you bought from a guy at the traffic light? Nope.

GET ROMANTIC

Is there a certain unique phrase you and your spouse say to one another? (Example: I love you forever and don't you forget it!) Make it an acronym: ILYFADYFI. Congratulations! You now have a secret code to text each other at regular intervals. (See p. 119 for more ideas.)

LOVE LESSON

Be sincere when you praise your spouse. Say good things you really mean, and say them a lot.

27

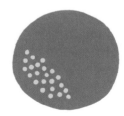

DATE NIGHT

If it's warm enough and light enough outside, head to the local driving range after dinner. It doesn't matter if both of you play golf. Even if the sport is completely foreign to you both, hack away with gusto. It'll be fun.

The investment we put into

BUILDING

our marriages
is one of the best
investments we can
possibly make.

— Jimmy Evans

GET ROMANTIC

Husbands: Foot rubs are not just for pedicurists. You don't have to be an expert to give one, and she'll love you for it.

Wives: Your husband would love a foot rub, too. He probably just doesn't know it.

LOVE LESSON

When you and your spouse disagree, work hard to listen and understand. Empathy is more important than winning an argument.

28

DEEPER

When you and your spouse head out for a date, enjoy the conversation, but try to steer clear of discussions about the usual stuff, like the kids, work, finances, and other touchy subjects. A date is your chance to escape from the everyday. Save those topics for another time. (For some good escape-worthy conversation starters, check out p. 118.)

When was the last time you dressed up together for a night out? Do it regardless of your destination. Do it for no reason other than to look nice and feel special—and to make everyone else wonder what you're up to.

GET ROMANTIC

If the only time you give your spouse a greeting card is on holidays or birthdays, then fix that immediately. Spontaneous Card Day!

LOVE LESSON

When arguing with your spouse about something, stay focused on the issue itself. Never attack the person. Always fight fair. This means no yelling, exaggerating, or getting defensive. Also no medieval weaponry, but that should go without saying.

29

DEEPER

Start each day by asking yourself how you will show love to your spouse. Then follow that lead. At the end of the day, reflect. How successful were you?

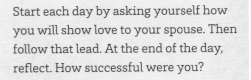

DATE NIGHT

Go to one of those do-it-yourself
ceramic painting places. Paint
a coffee mug or plate for each
other. Extra credit for hiding a
secret message inside the mug or
underneath the plate! (No paint-
your-own-pottery studios near
you? Then browse over to a DIY site
like Instructables.com and make
something together.)

GET ROMANTIC

Wives, he will absolutely go shopping with you if you promise to let him pick out something slinky for you to wear.

LOVE LESSON

Marriages deteriorate like muscles. You're not guaranteed a good marriage just because it was healthy for two or three years. You always have to work at things like communication, conflict management, and thoughtfulness. Without discipline and commitment, your marriage will get flabby.

30

DEEPER

A strong, happy marriage is characterized by positive words. Discipline yourself to start making more positive statements about your spouse and relationship. Hint: "I'm absolutely positive you're wrong" does not count.

When was the last time you laughed with your spouse? If you can't remember, then watch one of your favorite comedies or TV shows together, or attend a live comedy performance.

laugh

GET ROMANTIC

When was the last time you served your spouse breakfast in bed? If you can't remember, then guess what? Now you have plans for Saturday!

LOVE LESSON

Great marriages are the result of two people who go through challenging or difficult times and find a way to stay together—and even grow closer—through the process.

31

DATE NIGHT

Send the kids away for the night. Stay home. Play their video games. Laugh like 6-year-olds. (But don't tell the kids.)

Alternate responsibilities for your date nights. One week, he plans. The next week, it's her job. Try to outdo each other.

Next weekend's date (HIM):

This weekend's date (HER):

Classic novels of romance

There's a big difference between a novel of romance and a romance novel. Find a classic that fits the first category and you'll love reading it out loud to your spouse. Find a trashier entry in the second category and you'll not be able to read because of the giggling. Or blushing. Or abject shame.

It's best to go with Category One. Here are a few classics known for their romantic stories and distinct lack of trashiness:

* *Little Women*, by Louisa May Alcott
* *Jane Eyre*, by Charlotte Brontë
* *Wuthering Heights*, by Emily Brontë
* *Pride and Prejudice*, by Jane Austen
* *Anna Karenina*, by Leo Tolstoy
* *Gone with the Wind*, by Margaret Mitchell
* *The Phantom of the Opera*, by Gaston Leroux
* *Doctor Zhivago*, by Boris Pasternak
* *The Great Gatsby*, by F. Scott Fitzgerald

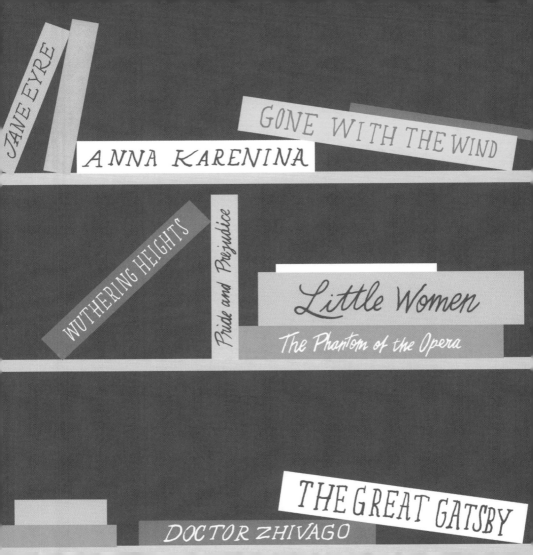

GET ROMANTIC

Mail your spouse a "thank you" card to his or her place of business. Inside, list the many things you're thankful for.

LOVE LESSON

The best gift you can give your children is to love their mom or dad.

32

DATE NIGHT

Kites are not just for idyllic childhood memories and Norman Rockwell paintings. Pick up an inexpensive one at the local discount store and head to the park. Take turns.

Love means acting in one another's best interests REGARDLESS of how you feel.

— Jimmy Evans

How to write a love letter

Trouble putting words to your feelings? Try using this as a template:

Dear *(name)*,

When we got married *(insert number)* years ago, you made me the luckiest *(noun indicating gender)* alive. You mean the world to me.

I love the way you *(something great your spouse does)*. I am so grateful for your *(positive attribute #1)*, *(positive attribute #2)*, and *(positive attribute #3)*. And it doesn't hurt that you're so incredibly *(beautiful/handsome, depending on gender)*.

Thank you for being you, and thank you for putting up with me.

I love you forever...
(your name here)

Dear

I love you forever...

GET ROMANTIC

This week, pick one of your spouse's regular chores and do it for him or her. (Mow the lawn. Do the laundry. Clean the garage. Dust.)

LOVE LESSON

One thing that warms the heart of any husband or wife is knowing your spouse is tuned in to your needs and concerns. When you're with your spouse, be present. Pay attention. Don't allow yourself to get distracted.

33

DEEPER

Nothing bonds a couple—or is naturally more romantic—than the intimacy of sharing a private joke. Find ways to cultivate them and laugh together.

Does your city still have a drive-in movie theater? Kick it old school and give it a try. Extra points if you drive a convertible.

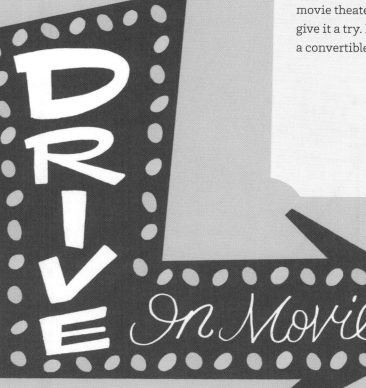

GET ROMANTIC

After you come home from work, always greet your spouse with a hug and a kiss. Always. Even in front of the kids. Even if it makes them squirm.

LOVE LESSON

Four verbs to avoid for a good marriage: *Blame, Complain, Criticize, Nag.*

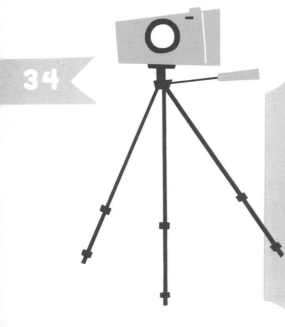

34

DATE NIGHT

Get a tripod and digital camera. Go out on the town. Photograph yourselves with signs, people and/or objects whose names begin with each letter of the alphabet. A to Z. No quitting early!

God designed

marriage

to be a total sharing of life
between two people, and it's
worth the sacrifice.

— Jimmy Evans

GET ROMANTIC

Hold hands often. When you pray. When you walk together. When you watch TV. When you talk.

LOVE LESSON

Three rules for a successful life with your spouse:

1) Honor and accept your differences.
2) Work hard to meet each other's needs.
3) Communicate with honesty, kindness, and understanding.

35

DEEPER

Healthy married couples don't get married for personal gain. You swear fidelity to each other, not to yourself.

Make dessert. Get all the supplies ahead of time, then bake and decorate a cake together. Or make cookies. Or decorate a cake with a bunch of cookies. Then, together, enjoy your delicious decadence.

GET ROMANTIC

Stop turning to the same old clichés when you shop for a romantic gift. Instead, think of something that matches up with your spouse's hobbies or interests. Save for it, buy it, wrap it, and give it out of the blue. Romance is about unexpected surprise and delight.

LOVE LESSON

Sometimes arguments can be beneficial, but only to resolve an issue. Don't start one just to blow smoke or be mean.

36

DATE NIGHT

Today's couples see their friends less frequently than couples did a few decades ago. On your next date night, plan something with friends. Take a gourmet cooking class. Go bowling. Engage in a husbands vs. wives paintball war.

The most meaningful romance is the *educated romance* born of **selflessness, choice,** and **discipline.**

— Jimmy Evans

GET ROMANTIC

When was the last time you sat down with your spouse to watch your wedding video or look at wedding photos? Relive the magic (without the stress).

LOVE LESSON

Behind the healthiest marriages are husbands and wives willing to sacrifice for each other. A husband who serves his wife becomes much more attractive to her. A wife who gives generously to her husband will be met with a faithful, committed spouse. Lay down your life for your mate and you'll find the marriage you've been seeking.

37

DEEPER

Any time a conflict arises and the time comes to discuss it—in other words, when a fight breaks out—kick things off by affirming your love and commitment to the relationship. Set a healing tone from the start.

DATE NIGHT

Sure, you could go on a coffee date to Starbucks. But why not brew your own, fill a Thermos®, bundle up, and head to the park?

Love poems

GET ROMANTIC

Bring home fresh flowers... but in a pot, with roots. As soon as you can, the two of you can plant them outside.

LOVE LESSON

Remember how much affection you showed each other when your relationship first got serious? The natural tendency is for affection to diminish as the years go by. Don't let this happen.

38

DATE NIGHT

Set aside an evening without kids and clean out your closets together. Pick out the stuff you haven't worn in awhile. Model it for your spouse. If it doesn't get a thumbs-up and you don't want it, donate it to a local charity.

you only

SUCCEED

in relationships to the proportion that you

WORK *at them.*

— Jimmy Evans

GET ROMANTIC

The next time you get a chance, take a walk together after dinner. Stroll around the neighborhood, to a local park, or to the nearest coffee shop. You don't need a destination. Just enjoy the time with your spouse.

LOVE LESSON

Nothing transforms a marriage like selfless, sacrificial love. Put each other first. Serve your spouse. Consider his or her needs above your own.

39

Take a Walk

DATE NIGHT

TV show binge: pick up the DVD or stream a television show you never got around to watching. View several episodes in a row (without commercials!).

What's her favorite meal? What's his favorite athlete or team? What's your spouse's best childhood memory or favorite family vacation spot? If you don't know the answers to these questions, ask. Then remember.

GET ROMANTIC

If you can, plan a time this week when you both can step away from work or home and meet somewhere for coffee (or your favorite daytime beverage). No agenda. Just enjoy hanging out.

LOVE LESSON

Romance is easiest at the start of marriage, because everything is new and fresh and exciting. It gets harder after a few years have passed, as you both settle into the routines of your life together. This is when romance becomes most important. Commit to it. Practice it. Be intentional about it!

40

DEEPER

Make a goal for the next calendar year: Find at least three bed-and-breakfasts in your area, within an hour's drive. Try each of them out for a night.

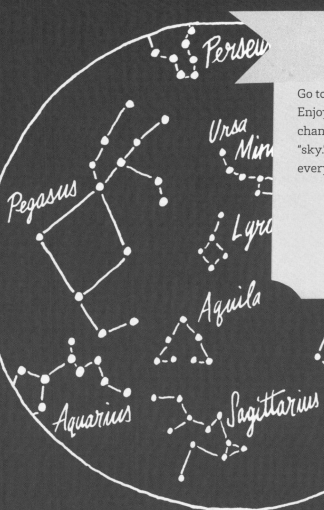

DATE NIGHT

Go to your local planetarium. Enjoy the show...and also enjoy the chance to cuddle under the dark "sky." Extra credit: you must kiss every time you hear the word *orbit*.

GET ROMANTIC

Write I L-O-V-E Y-O-U on eight individual notecards. Scatter them where your spouse will find them throughout the day. Will he or she get the message?

LOVE LESSON

No one expects married couples to like all the same things. It's perfectly acceptable to maintain unique interests and hobbies. Two rules: First, always respect the things your spouse likes—never belittle them. Second, be careful with the time you set aside for your "stuff." Don't let it overtake the time devoted to your marriage.

41

DEEPER

Do you say "I love you" to your spouse every day? Because you should. Bonus round: Try to compliment your spouse as often as you say "I love you." It takes a little more effort, but is so worthwhile.

Cupcake taste test: Head to your local bakery, buy a variety of the day's offerings, and try a bite of each for dessert.

GET ROMANTIC

Sure, you can use windshield wipers to get the rain off, but they're also ideal for securing surprise love notes.

LOVE LESSON

Hearing is a physical function of the ear. It's something that happens whether you want it to or not. But listening is different. Listening is an intellectual devotion to what you hear, and it is your choice. Do you only hear your spouse? Or do you listen?

42

DEEPER

Romance isn't something that just happens. You can't wait for it to find its way into your marriage. Whether you're the husband or the wife, you have to make it happen on a regular basis. Be disciplined about it. Make it a priority.

Schedule a do-it-yourself outdoor date night at home. Husbands, grill up the meat and veggies. Wives, bake bread and make the dessert. Set up a table and enjoy some open-air dining in the backyard.

Kiss the cook

GET ROMANTIC

As soon as you get a chance, finish this statement with a text or email to your spouse: "I love how you _____."

LOVE LESSON

Stop doing the things that drive your spouse crazy. You know there are certain things that irritate the daylights out of him or her. So why not just stop doing those things? Put the toilet seat down. Lay off the nagging. Pick up your clothes. Stick to your budget.

43

DATE NIGHT

Buy theater or concert tickets in advance and then mail them to your spouse, along with a formal invitation to your night out.

Most of us think in our own male or female emotional "language." To succeed in marriage you must be emotionally bilingual. Study how your spouse deals with things like criticism, stress, or challenges—then communicate accordingly.

Communicate

Amusing things to whisper into your spouse's ear

Next time you're at a party, at church, at your spouse's workplace, or otherwise standing beside your husband or wife in a public place, whisper in his or her ear. Lean in so close that your lips graze flesh. Try one of these fun, intimate phrases and enjoy the reaction:

* "I love you."
* "I want you."
* "Tonight I'm yours."
* "You look spectacular."
* "Let's get out of here."
* "Wanna go home with me?"
* "Wanna make out?"

How to praise your spouse

Kind words and appreciation are foundational for a good, healthy relationship, and everyone likes a compliment. But sometimes it's hard to know what to say.

If you struggle to put words to your feelings—*ahem*, MEN—try these fill-in-the-blank prompts. Wives, these are for you, too.

All parties should use these phrases frequently:

✳ Thank you so much for _____.

✳ I love it when you _____.

✳ The thing I admire most about you is _____.

✳ It really makes me happy when you _____.

✳ That really impressed me when you _____.

✳ I know you love me when you _____.

✳ I wish I were as good at _____ as you are.

✳ You look smokin' hot in that/those _____.

GET ROMANTIC

Write him a love note tomorrow and hide it in his pants pocket... or his car... or his briefcase... or his gym bag. Write her a love note tomorrow and hide it in her purse... or her car... or on her mirror.

LOVE LESSON

Resolve to be honest when communicating with your spouse. Hiding your feelings can turn into a kind of willful dishonesty. One good rule to follow: When one spouse senses something is bothering the other and asks what's wrong, never accept "nothing" as an answer. It's never "nothing." It's always something. Spill the beans.

44

DEEPER

If you have kids, know that they are learning about marriage by watching how you do it...all the time. Don't ever forget this.

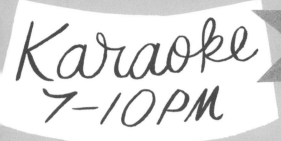

Karaoke 7–10PM

DATE NIGHT

Have you and your spouse ever tried karaoke for a date night? Set aside your inhibitions, pick a good duet, and let loose.

GET ROMANTIC

When you give an unexpected gift to your spouse, it's not the gift itself that is meaningful. It's the fact that you know your husband or wife has been thinking about you.

LOVE LESSON

Romance is not a seasonal extra or obligation for Valentine's Day. It should be a part of your daily life. Every marriage desperately needs it.

45

DATE NIGHT

Use your smartphone or GPS device to go geocaching together. What's geocaching? It's an outdoor, real-life treasure-hunting game where you try to find hidden containers marked with specific GPS coordinates. Check out a site like geocaching.com to get the coordinates for a treasure hidden near you.

The way you become a

soulmate

with someone is by
going through

DIFFICULTY

together.

— Jimmy Evans

DINNER OUT Again?

There will be times in a marriage when any kind of date night seems like a luxury. It's enough to just get away from everything for awhile. But there will be other times when you seem to fall into a rut. Yet another restaurant meal? Keep it fresh! Add some zest to dinner out with one of these ideas:

* If you're tired of the same-old local restaurant fare, pick a small town at least 30 miles away, and drive there for dinner.
* Go to your favorite restaurant but don't sit across from each other, like usual. Sit side-by-side.
* Go spontaneous. Toss options for 1) restaurant and 2) activities (movie, dessert, coffee) into a hat and choose at random.
* During the week, find a small "hole in the wall" restaurant where you've never eaten before. Then take your spouse there. Enjoy the little adventure!
* Take your spouse to a favorite restaurant, but you're not allowed to order an entree. Appetizers only (more than one if necessary). Try something new.
* Try a new restaurant, but with a catch: You have to order for each other. How well do you know your spouse?
* Pick a restaurant more than a mile away and walk there together. The approach will build up your appetite. The walk home will aid your digestion!

Small-town DINER

GET ROMANTIC

Every day, try to surprise your spouse with an unexpected show of affection. A spontaneous hug. A surprise whisper in the ear. A sudden, public kiss on the lips. (Guys: Make sure you do it in a way that thrills rather than embarrasses your wife. Women: Doesn't matter how, where, or why you do it. He'll love it.)

LOVE LESSON

Show interest in the things your spouse is interested in. Even fantasy football? Yes. Even shopping? Yes. Even (fill in the blank)? Yes.

46

DATE NIGHT

Treat each other to a couple's massage at a local spa. Yes, it can be expensive, but you can bond while you're being pampered. Relaxing and romantic.

With your spouse, take a hard look at your own marriage... then compare your relationship to your parents' and in-laws' marriages. What traits do they share? What deficiencies? Don't miss the fact that, by virtue of personality and upbringing, your marriage may look similar to theirs in a couple of decades. If you need to make any course adjustments, now's the time to do it.

Conversation Starters

You're on a date with your spouse or are otherwise enjoying precious time to yourself. You don't want to talk about the usual stuff—the kids, the house, or your jobs. You just want to talk.

To spark good conversation, here are some questions to ask each other:

* If we could go back and change it, would you have wanted a longer or shorter engagement? Why?
* What would you have changed about our wedding ceremony or reception?
* What do you wish I was better at?
* Where would you like our relationship to be in five years?
* What do you think we'll do after the kids have moved out? Or after we retire?
* How have we changed the most since our first year of marriage?
* If the two of us could travel anywhere in the world together, where would you want to go?
* If I were to die, would you want to get remarried? (Yes, this might lead to a heavy conversation—and possibly a difficult one—but it could also be incredibly meaningful.)

Handy guide to Secret texting acronyms

Need some overly complicated texting acronyms for intimate spousal communication? Of course you do! Try these...

* **YATOOFM**: You are the only one for me.

* **HAGDH**: Have a great day, honey!

* **CWFYTGH**: Can't wait for you to get home.

* **IMYVVM**: I miss you very, very much.

* **HGL**: Hey, good-lookin'.

* **BKTYFM**: Big kiss to you from me.

* **CTADH**: Consider this a digital hug.

* **GRIHPFYTY!**: Get ready. I have plans for you tonight. Yowza!

* **IIIIIWALY**: I... will always love you (as if sung by Dolly Parton or Whitney Houston)

GET ROMANTIC

Hold hands, but arrange them differently. Does your hand go in front of your spouse's or behind it? Do you intertwine fingers? Try it, even if it feels awkward. A re-positioning allows you to experienced your husband or wife's familiar hand in a brand-new way.

LOVE LESSON

You're both adults, but it's important to respect the wisdom and advice of your parents...and in-laws. Be gracious toward the generation that came before you.

47

DATE NIGHT

Drive to an unfamiliar (but safe) neighborhood. Park your car, then explore together on foot. If there are restaurants or coffee shops nearby, give them a try. Enjoying new experiences together is a great way to deepen your relationship.

DEEPER

A marriage begins to go bad when a
wife or husband

NO LONGER
FEELS VALUED.

— Jimmy Evans

GET ROMANTIC

Make your next kiss last longer than expected.

LOVE LESSON

Love is a lot of things, but one aspect of it is emotional. It has to do with the way you feel when you're with a certain person: You feel good when you're with them. Do your words, behaviors, and attitudes trigger those good feelings in your spouse? If not, then maybe it's time for some personal changes.

48

DEEPER

It takes effort to create romance in your marriage. You have to be creative. You have to dedicate time to it. You have to plan ahead and make sacrifices. But the benefits of creating romance in your marriage far outweigh the effort.

DATE NIGHT

Leave work early and head to the farmer's market together. Buy produce together. Make a fresh salad together. Get fresh together (optional but recommended).

GET ROMANTIC

Most guys don't want a bouquet of flowers, but a bouquet of cookies? Now you're talking.

LOVE LESSON

If a conflict arises, try not to let it fester. Discuss it as soon as possible. If you don't clear the air soon enough, you'll be feeding resentment. When you do talk it out, speak gently to your husband or wife. Sharp or loud voices rarely are helpful.

49

Thai
Ethiopian
Korean BBQ
Mexican
Japanese
Jamaican

DATE NIGHT

List your favorite ethnic foods (Indian, Thai, Tex-Mex, etc.). Then date your way through the list, trying a new restaurant each time.

Love is a commodity that cannot be STORED. It can only be experienced today.

— Jimmy Evans

GET ROMANTIC

Sharing ice cream is romantic. *Idea #1:* Buy a small container of your favorite flavor. Split it on a park bench. (Don't forget the spoons.) *Idea #2:* Pretend you're in a classic sitcom. Share a milkshake with two straws! *Idea #3:* Split a banana split. Start on each end, and meet in the middle.

LOVE LESSON

What phrase do wives always like to hear from their husbands? "What can I do to help?"

What phrase do husbands like to hear from their wives? "You did such a great job!"

50

DATE NIGHT

Indulge in some culture together. Visit a local art gallery or museum. Catch a play at the community theater. Know any musicians in a local band? Find out when they play next, and make a date to see them.

Exercise together. Go on plenty of walks. Be spotters for each other or take a class together at the gym. Sign up for a 5K and train for it together. Never underestimate the, uh, hormonal value of sweating with your spouse. You'll be pleasantly surprised.

Running Log

GET ROMANTIC

Show as much as you tell. Saying "I love you" is vitally important, but so are the actions that speak for themselves. In fact, words are meaningless if they aren't backed up by deeds. Think of an action that says "I love you" and do it!

LOVE LESSON

It's acceptable to drop hints or leave reminder notes every now and then, especially if you have a forgetful spouse. But don't nag. Nagging is when the reminders don't let up and the faultfinding never stops.

51

DATE NIGHT

Picnic surprise: Each of you is in charge of secretly packing a picnic meal for the other. No fast food allowed! Find a nice, peaceful park and enjoy the surprise.

one good word can open the hardest door.

There's an old saying: *one good word can open the hardest door.* The next time you get a chance, tell your spouse something you love about him or her.

GET ROMANTIC

The most romantic gestures are small, unexpected things. A flower for no reason. A love note out of nowhere. A surprise gift.

LOVE LESSON

Think of marriage as a "giving contest." Whoever gives and serves the most wins. So pour on the personal generosity, knowing that if you "win," your spouse wins, too.

52

DEEPER

Advice for married couples: Don't "give advice" to your spouse. After all, how well do you personally deal with correction?

Ten Questions

Plan a night for just the two of you, then each of you come up with 10 questions you want to ask the other. Choose a location where you'll be free to have a long, uninterrupted conversation. Ask away, answer honestly, and enjoy a wide-open opportunity to communicate.

Questions to ask your spouse every day

Good communication is vital to a successful marriage. Showing interest in your spouse by asking questions about what's going on in their life isn't just about being polite. It's a way of connecting with each other and sharing life together.

Reminder for men: Your wife deserves more than one-word answers to these questions.

Reminder for women: First allow your husband time to decompress. He doesn't want to be interrogated at the door.

Questions to ask every morning before you leave each other:
* What's going on today?
* What are you looking forward to?
* Is there anything I can do for you today?

Questions to ask every evening:
* What was the best thing that happened to you today?
* What was the most challenging part of your day?
* What do you wish you had done differently?

This Paper Ship is Joel and Ashley Selby, a husband-and-wife freelance illustration and creative team. They started working together as art school sweethearts, meeting during a fabric study in Drawing 101. At first they competed against each other in design classes, though they often worked on each others' projects, which sometimes backfired when one of them got a better grade than the other.

When they graduated in 2009 to a bad economy and few job prospects, they took up their pencils and brushes side-by-side again to set sail as This Paper Ship, and in 2011 were blessed to launch into freelancing together full time. Working for Marriage Today on *Happy, Happy Love* was a double blessing: practicing their drawing skills while learning to be a happier married couple.

They live in central North Carolina and at www.thispapership.com.

Photograph by Molly Flanagan (mollyflanagan.com)